This fuckin' book belongs to:

_____

Date : _____

Fucks Given Today

0   1   2   3   4   5   6   7   8   9   10

Punk ass coworkers I hate

Shit my boss did to piss me off

Fuck This Shitshow

Shit I rather be doing

Punch in the face before I quit list

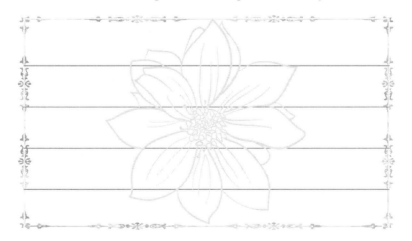

Celebrations

Coworker's that didn't get cussed out

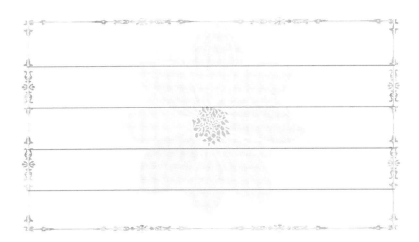

Shit I thought but didn't say

Date : _____

Fucks Given Today

0   1   2   3   4   5   6   7   8   9   10

Punk ass coworkers I hate

Shit my boss did to piss me off

Fuck This Job

Shit I rather be doing

Punch in the face before I quit list

Celebrations

Coworker's that didn't get cussed out

Shit I thought but didn't say

Date : _____

Fucks Given Today

0   1   2   3   4   5   6   7   8   9   10

Punk ass coworkers I hate

Shit my boss did to piss me off

Fuck This Job

Shit I rather be doing

Punch in the face before I quit list

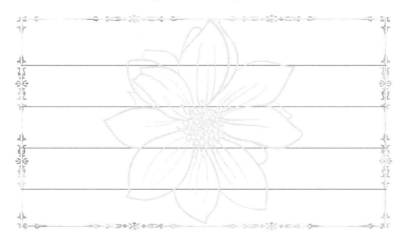

Celebrations

Coworker's that didn't get cussed out

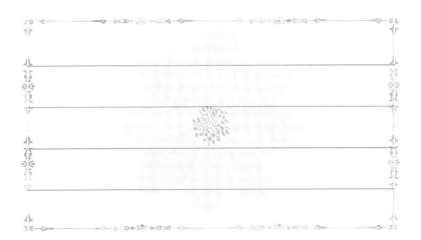

Shit I thought but didn't say

Date : _____

Fucks Given Today

0   1   2   3   4   5   6   7   8   9   10

Punk ass coworkers I hate

Shit my boss did to piss me off

Fuck This Job

Shit I rather be doing

Punch in the face before I quit list

Celebrations

Coworker's that didn't get cussed out

Shit I thought but didn't say

Date : _____

Fucks Given Today

0   1   2   3   4   5   6   7   8   9   10

Punk ass coworkers I hate

Shit my boss did to piss me off

Fuck This Job

Shit I rather be doing

Punch in the face before I quit list

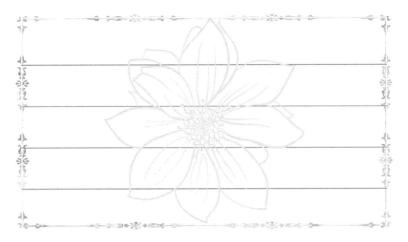

Celebrations

Coworker's that didn't get cussed out

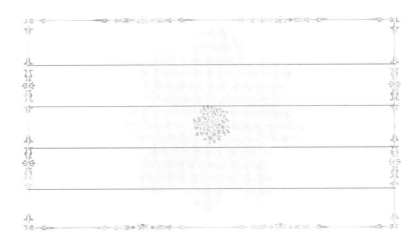

Shit I thought but didn't say

Date : _____

Fucks Given Today

0 1 2 3 4 5 6 7 8 9 10

Punk ass coworkers I hate

Shit my boss did to piss me off

Fuck This Job

Shit I rather be doing

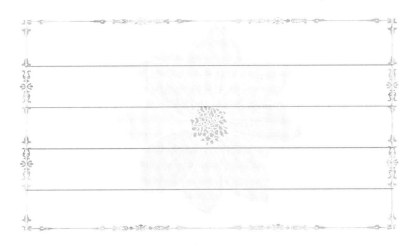

Punch in the face before I quit list

Celebrations

Coworker's that didn't get cussed out

Shit I thought but didn't say

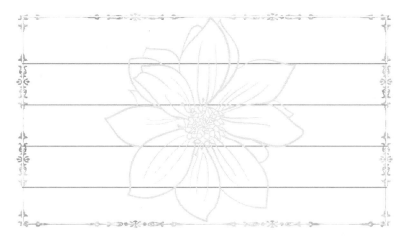

Date : _____

Fucks Given Today

0   1   2   3   4   5   6   7   8   9   10

Punk ass coworkers I hate

Shit my boss did to piss me off

Fuck This Job

Shit I rather be doing

Punch in the face before I quit list

Celebrations

Coworker's that didn't get cussed out

Shit I thought but didn't say

Date : _____

Fucks Given Today

0   1   2   3   4   5   6   7   8   9   10

Punk ass coworkers I hate

Shit my boss did to piss me off

Fuck This Job

Shit I rather be doing

Punch in the face before I quit list

Celebrations

Coworker's that didn't get cussed out

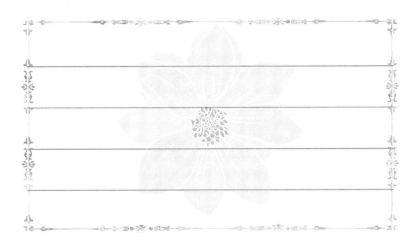

Shit I thought but didn't say

Date : _____

Fucks Given Today

0   1   2   3   4   5   6   7   8   9   10

Punk ass coworkers I hate

Shit my boss did to piss me off

Fuck This Job

Shit I rather be doing

Punch in the face before I quit list

Celebrations

Coworker's that didn't get cussed out

Shit I thought but didn't say

Date : _____

Fucks Given Today

0   1   2   3   4   5   6   7   8   9   10

Punk ass coworkers I hate

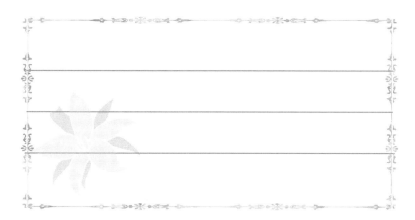

Shit my boss did to piss me off

Fuck This Job

Shit I rather be doing

Punch in the face before I quit list

Celebrations

Coworker's that didn't get cussed out

Shit I thought but didn't say

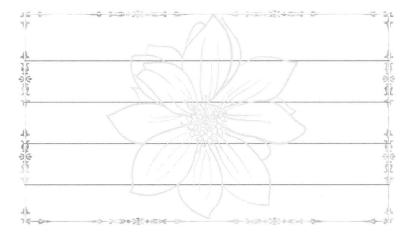

Date : _____

Fucks Given Today

0   1   2   3   4   5   6   7   8   9   10

Punk ass coworkers I hate

Shit my boss did to piss me off

Fuck This Job

Shit I rather be doing

Punch in the face before I quit list

Celebrations

Coworker's that didn't get cussed out

Shit I thought but didn't say

Date : _____

Fucks Given Today

0   1   2   3   4   5   6   7   8   9   10

Punk ass coworkers I hate

Shit my boss did to piss me off

Fuck This Job

Shit I rather be doing

Punch in the face before I quit list

Celebrations

Coworker's that didn't get cussed out

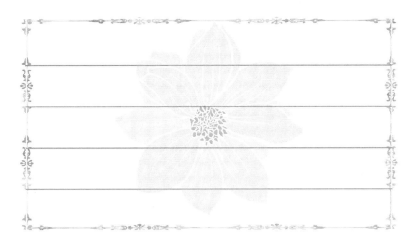

Shit I thought but didn't say

Date : _____

Fucks Given Today

0   1   2   3   4   5   6   7   8   9   10

Punk ass coworkers I hate

Shit my boss did to piss me off

Fuck This Job

Shit I rather be doing

Punch in the face before I quit list

Celebrations

Coworker's that didn't get cussed out

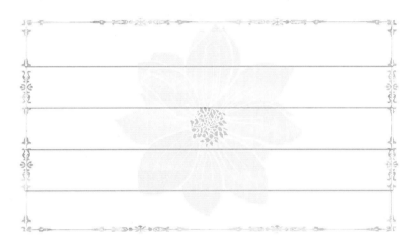

Shit I thought but didn't say

Date : _____

Fucks Given Today

0   1   2   3   4   5   6   7   8   9   10

Punk ass coworkers I hate

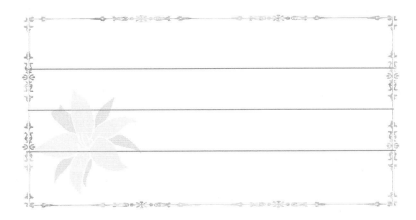

Shit my boss did to piss me off

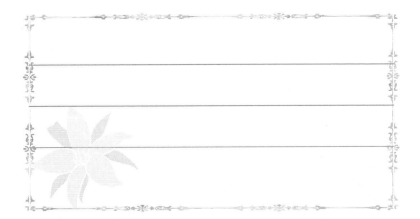

Fuck This Job

Shit I rather be doing

Punch in the face before I quit list

Celebrations

Coworker's that didn't get cussed out

Shit I thought but didn't say

Date : _____

Fucks Given Today

0　1　2　3　4　5　6　7　8　9　10

Punk ass coworkers I hate

Shit my boss did to piss me off

Fuck This Job

Shit I rather be doing

Punch in the face before I quit list

Celebrations

Coworker's that didn't get cussed out

Shit I thought but didn't say

Date : _____

Fucks Given Today

0   1   2   3   4   5   6   7   8   9   10

Punk ass coworkers I hate

Shit my boss did to piss me off

Fuck This Job

Shit I rather be doing

Punch in the face before I quit list

Celebrations

Coworker's that didn't get cussed out

Shit I thought but didn't say

Date : _____

Fucks Given Today

0   1   2   3   4   5   6   7   8   9   10

Punk ass coworkers I hate

Shit my boss did to piss me off

Fuck This Job

Shit I rather be doing

Punch in the face before I quit list

Celebrations

Coworker's that didn't get cussed out

Shit I thought but didn't say

Date : _____

Fucks Given Today

0   1   2   3   4   5   6   7   8   9   10

Punk ass coworkers I hate

Shit my boss did to piss me off

Fuck This Job

Shit I rather be doing

Punch in the face before I quit list

Celebrations

Coworker's that didn't get cussed out

Shit I thought but didn't say

Date : _____

Fucks Given Today

0   1   2   3   4   5   6   7   8   9   10

Punk ass coworkers I hate

Shit my boss did to piss me off

Fuck This Job

Shit I rather be doing

Punch in the face before I quit list

Celebrations

Coworker's that didn't get cussed out

Shit I thought but didn't say

Date : _____

Fucks Given Today

0   1   2   3   4   5   6   7   8   9   10

Punk ass coworkers I hate

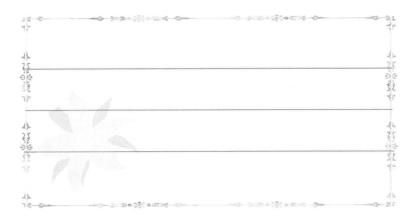

Shit my boss did to piss me off

Fuck This Job

Shit I rather be doing

Punch in the face before I quit list

Celebrations

Coworker's that didn't get cussed out

Shit I thought but didn't say

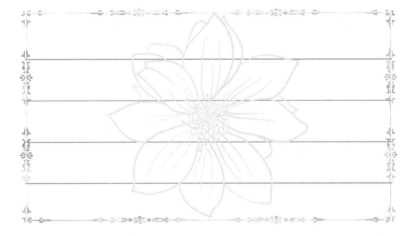

Date : _____

Fucks Given Today

0   1   2   3   4   5   6   7   8   9   10

Punk ass coworkers I hate

Shit my boss did to piss me off

Fuck This Job

Shit I rather be doing

Punch in the face before I quit list

Celebrations

Coworker's that didn't get cussed out

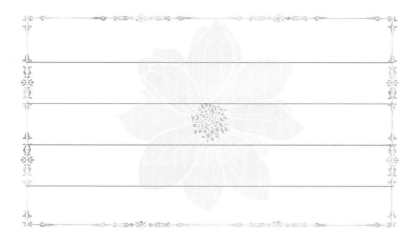

Shit I thought but didn't say

Date : _____

Fucks Given Today

0 1 2 3 4 5 6 7 8 9 10

Punk ass coworkers I hate

Shit my boss did to piss me off

Fuck This Job

Shit I rather be doing

Punch in the face before I quit list

Celebrations

Coworker's that didn't get cussed out

Shit I thought but didn't say

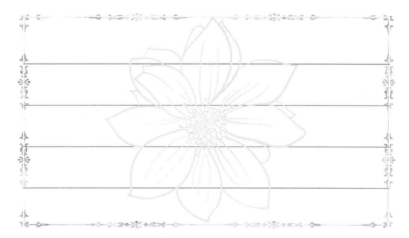

Date : _____

Fucks Given Today

0   1   2   3   4   5   6   7   8   9   10

Punk ass coworkers I hate

Shit my boss did to piss me off

Fuck This Job

Shit I rather be doing

Punch in the face before I quit list

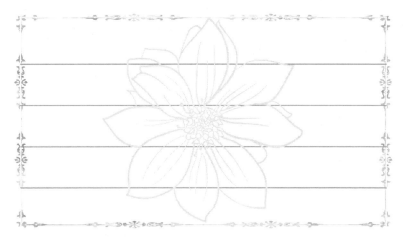

Celebrations

Coworker's that didn't get cussed out

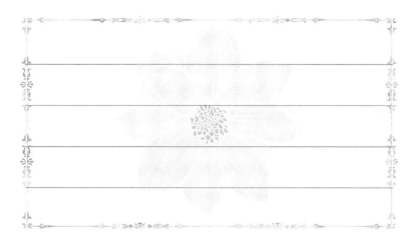

Shit I thought but didn't say

Date : _____

Fucks Given Today

0 1 2 3 4 5 6 7 8 9 10

Punk ass coworkers I hate

Shit my boss did to piss me off

Fuck This Job

Shit I rather be doing

Punch in the face before I quit list

Celebrations

Coworker's that didn't get cussed out

Shit I thought but didn't say

Date : _____

Fucks Given Today

0   1   2   3   4   5   6   7   8   9   10

Punk ass coworkers I hate

Shit my boss did to piss me off

Fuck This Job

Shit I rather be doing

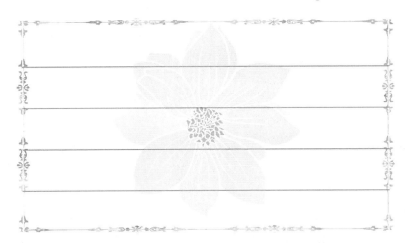

Punch in the face before I quit list

Celebrations

Coworker's that didn't get cussed out

Shit I thought but didn't say

Date : _____

Fucks Given Today

0   1   2   3   4   5   6   7   8   9   10

Punk ass coworkers I hate

Shit my boss did to piss me off

Fuck This Job

Shit I rather be doing

Punch in the face before I quit list

Celebrations

Coworker's that didn't get cussed out

Shit I thought but didn't say

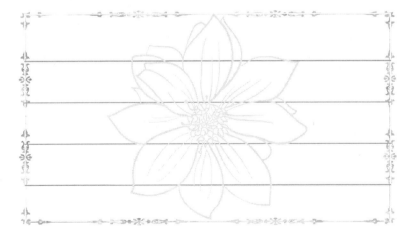

Date : _____

Fucks Given Today

0   1   2   3   4   5   6   7   8   9   10

Punk ass coworkers I hate

Shit my boss did to piss me off

Fuck This Job

Shit I rather be doing

Punch in the face before I quit list

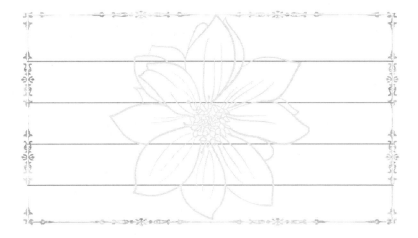

Celebrations

Coworker's that didn't get cussed out

Shit I thought but didn't say

Date : _____

Fucks Given Today

0   1   2   3   4   5   6   7   8   9   10

Punk ass coworkers I hate

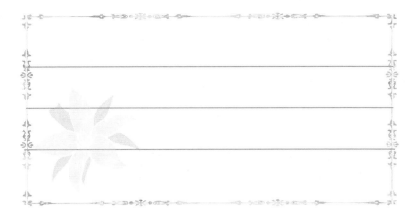

Shit my boss did to piss me off

Fuck This Job

Shit I rather be doing

Punch in the face before I quit list

Celebrations

Coworker's that didn't get cussed out

Shit I thought but didn't say

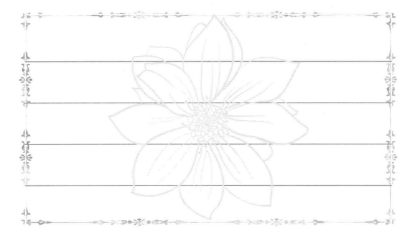

Date : _____

Fucks Given Today

0   1   2   3   4   5   6   7   8   9   10

Punk ass coworkers I hate

Shit my boss did to piss me off

Fuck This Job

Shit I rather be doing

Punch in the face before I quit list

Celebrations

Coworker's that didn't get cussed out

Shit I thought but didn't say

Date : _____

Fucks Given Today

0   1   2   3   4   5   6   7   8   9   10

Punk ass coworkers I hate

Shit my boss did to piss me off

Fuck This Job

Shit I rather be doing

Punch in the face before I quit list

Celebrations

Coworker's that didn't get cussed out

Shit I thought but didn't say

Date : _____

Fucks Given Today

0   1   2   3   4   5   6   7   8   9   10

Punk ass coworkers I hate

Shit my boss did to piss me off

Fuck This Job

Shit I rather be doing

Punch in the face before I quit list

Celebrations

Coworker's that didn't get cussed out

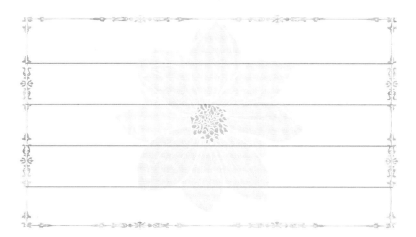

Shit I thought but didn't say

Date : _____

Fucks Given Today

0   1   2   3   4   5   6   7   8   9   10

Punk ass coworkers I hate

Shit my boss did to piss me off

Fuck This Job

Shit I rather be doing

Punch in the face before I quit list

Celebrations

Coworker's that didn't get cussed out

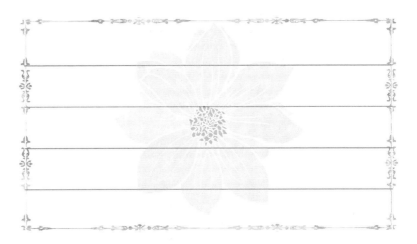

Shit I thought but didn't say

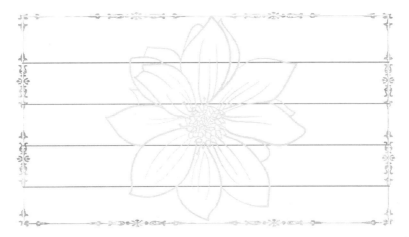

Date : _____

Fucks Given Today

0   1   2   3   4   5   6   7   8   9   10

Punk ass coworkers I hate

Shit my boss did to piss me off

Fuck This Job

Shit I rather be doing

Punch in the face before I quit list

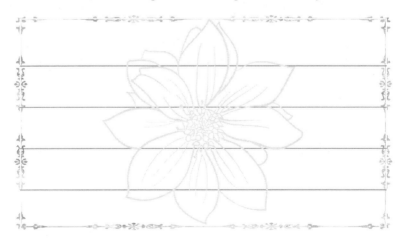

Celebrations

Coworker's that didn't get cussed out

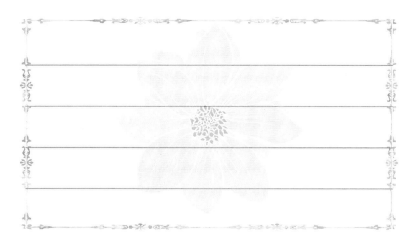

Shit I thought but didn't say

Date : _____

Fucks Given Today

0 1 2 3 4 5 6 7 8 9 10

Punk ass coworkers I hate

Shit my boss did to piss me off

Fuck This Job

Shit I rather be doing

Punch in the face before I quit list

Celebrations

Coworker's that didn't get cussed out

Shit I thought but didn't say

Date : _____

Fucks Given Today

0   1   2   3   4   5   6   7   8   9   10

Punk ass coworkers I hate

Shit my boss did to piss me off

Fuck This Job

Shit I rather be doing

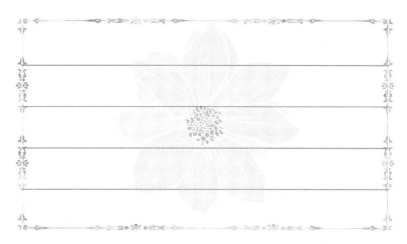

Punch in the face before I quit list

Celebrations

Coworker's that didn't get cussed out

Shit I thought but didn't say

Manufactured by Amazon.ca
Acheson, AB

11996332R00061